HAL LEONARD MELODICA METHOD

BY KATE VOSS

T0083078

PLAYBACK+
Speed • Pitch • Balance • Loop

To access audio visit:
www.halleonard.com/mylibrary

Enter Code
7087-7141-7193-8321

Page 3 Kate Voss photo: Don Stolley, used with permission.
Page 4 Button melodica photo: Evan Schiller, used with permission.

ISBN 978-1-70514-733-7

7777 W. BLUEMOUND RD. P.O. BOX 13819 MILWAUKEE, WI 53213

Copyright © 2023 by HAL LEONARD LLC
International Copyright Secured All Rights Reserved

No part of this publication may be reproduced in any form or by
any means without the prior written permission of the Publisher.

Visit Hal Leonard Online at
www.halleonard.com

World headquarters, contact:
Hal Leonard
7777 West Bluemound Road
Milwaukee, WI 53213
Email: info@halleonard.com

In Europe, contact:
Hal Leonard Europe Limited
1 Red Place
London, W1K 6PL
Email: info@halleonardeurope.com

In Australia, contact:
Hal Leonard Australia Pty. Ltd.
4 Lentara Court
Cheltenham, Victoria, 3192 Australia
Email: info@halleonard.com.au

Preface/About the Author.........................3

About the Melodica 4

Your Melodica (and How to Clean It!) 5

Fingering and Playing Positions 6

Mouthpiece Techniques and Breathing 7

    Articulation..................................8

    Rhythms......................................8

Notes on the Melodica 9

    The C-D-E Song...............................9

Musical Symbols and Notes on the Staff.........10

The Key of C 11

    Hot Dog Buns 11

    Mary Had A Little Lamb......................11

Dynamics.......................................12

    Are You Sleeping?...........................12

    Ode To Joy 12

Intervals 13

    Go Tell Aunt Rhody in Major and Minor 13

Half-steps, Sharps, Flats and Naturals 14

    In The Hall of the Mountain King 14

The Key of G 15

    Lightly Row.................................15

Key Signatures and Transposing 16

    Transposition Mission 16

Legato and Staccato............................17

    Are You Scary? 17

    Surprise Symphony 17

Eighth Notes 18

    Skip To My Lou 18

    Baby Bumblebee 18

Dotted Rhythms.................................19

    Row, Row, Row Your Boat.....................19

    Aloutte 19

Tied Notes 20

    Limehouse Blues 20

    My Bonnie Lies Over The Ocean...............21

Triplets 21

    Rockin' Triplets 21

Swing Rhythm 22

    Happy Birthday 22

The Key of F...................................23

    Twinkle, Twinkle Little Star................23

    Choucounne..................................23

Chromatic Scale................................24

    Entry of the Gladiators.....................24

    The Entertainer 25

Chords (and How to Read Them)..................26

    Chord Song 26

    Row, Row, Row Your Chords 26

Hush, Little Baby..............................27

    Chordially 27

Major and Minor Chords 28

    Molly Malone 28

Inversions 29

    Amazing Grace 29

    Triad Vocab 30

Bigger Chords..................................31

    7ths Song 31

    Nutcracker: March...........................32

Chord Groups 33

    Rockin' Chords..............................33

    Lavender's Blue (Chords and Melody).........34

    12-Bar Blues 34

Key of D.......................................35

    Minuet 35

Arpeggios 36

    Bugle Call 36

    Scarborough Fair 36

    Canon in D..................................37

Key of A 38

    Can Can.....................................38

The Blues Scale 39

    Play Along Blues 39

Improvising 41

    Mystery Melody 41

More Key Signatures 42

    Oh When The Saints Go Marching In 42

    Kumbaya.....................................42

    Lullaby 43

    Pop! Goes The Weasel 44

    Yankee Doodle 45

    Aura Lee 46

    Oh Danny Boy 47

Vibrato 48

    Ave Maria 49

Trills 50

    Peg O' My Heart 50

    Rondo Alla Turca 51

Rolls 52

    The House Of The Rising Sun 52

Glissando......................................53

    Darlene.....................................53

    Last Night Was The Last Time................54

Chord Chart 56

PREFACE

Why do we love music? For me, music is something that functions as a conductor of emotion. One of my favorite quotes that I first heard in high school and still resonates with me deeply today is one from French author Victor Hugo: "Music expresses that which cannot be said." Music is my comfort. It helps me process complex feelings. Music is my passion. It helps me reach my goals and dream big! Music is my muse. It helps me work hard and pushes me to try something new. Some people are so drawn to music that their entire lives are enveloped into it. Some people find it a relief and an aid to their lives. Some people simply enjoy it! Wherever you are on your musical journey, this book is meant to nurture your relationship with music and its rich history. There are infinite ways of expressing yourself musically — finding out what works best for YOU should be exploratory, joyful, interesting, exciting and at times frustrating. (Pro tip: Frustration is an excellent indicator that you are on the right track, passionate about what you are learning, AND more than likely on the verge of a breakthrough!) Doing what we love is an honor and a privilege and I hope the melodica can bring you as much joy as it has brought me. I would not have been able to write this book without the support of these amazing humans: Jason Goessl, Julie Waters, Carly Nelson, Peder Nelson, and Jenny McGlothern.

— Kate Voss

ABOUT THE AUTHOR

Kate "Sundae" Voss started playing piano at age 7 and has stayed active in the music scene ever since. It was evident from early on that performance was her main source of joy as she thrived in the choir and drama departments throughout school, earning awards and collecting scholarships as she went. Her dedication to music and performance continued to blossom after graduation when she became a full-time piano instructor at West Side Music Academy in Seattle. Quickly outgrowing her role as piano instructor, she worked with the owner to develop expansion of the school by offering lessons in multiple instruments and summer camps for students aged 3-18. All the while, Kate never stopped learning. She spent five years studying jazz vocals under the legendary Greta Matassa and jazz piano with Dick Cady while fine tuning her chops with local bands and jam sessions. When the melodica came into play (a gift from a friend in 2010) it was an easy sell with her jazz and pop groups, offering a new layer of sound and a little bit of gimmick. In 2013, Voss started a duo with Seattle guitarist, Jason Goessl focusing on pre-bop jazz with vocals, guitar and melodica called "Sundae + Mr. Goessl." When the duo took off in 2014, the gimmick of the melodica took a sharp turn to the forefront of the act, dazzling audiences with fluid and melodic playing. Crowds were so captivated by the instrument that the duo decided to sell melodicas as a merch item...since then the duo has sold over 300 instruments and Voss has become an Official Hohner Artist. Kate and Jason (now married) continue to tour and thrive with their duo and have settled in Oshkosh, WI with their rescue pup, Jackie Osassis. You can learn more about Sundae + Mr. Goessl at FunAndFancyMusic.com.

ABOUT THE MELODICA

Melodion, pianica, blow-keyboard, clavietta, melodihorn, wind piano, triola...these are some of the many terms for what is essentially the same instrument: the melodica! The melodica is an acoustic, breath-powered, free reed instrument with a keyboard attached. Imagine if an accordion and a harmonica had a baby, that bundle of joy would be the melodica. Because this instrument is multi-faceted, it belongs in a few different musical families. The sound is created by the breath flowing over a free reed, so it is considered a wind instrument *and* in the "free reed" family. Harmonicas, accordions, pump organs, melodicas and concertinas all use free reeds to produce their unique sounds. For the melodica, the reed plate sits underneath the keyboard, and when a key is pressed, a hole opens over the corresponding reed, allowing air from the breath to flow over the reed and produce a specific pitch. The sound reverberates out at an astonishing volume, making these instruments very popular in acoustic settings as well as on stage. Its small size makes it portable, and the piano keyboard makes it easy to learn and easy to play for students of all ages.

The melodica as we know it today has been around since the 1950s. In 1958, Hohner introduced a melodica that had buttons resembling piano keys and was played like a clarinet. While that style is still around today (mainly soprano and alto melodicas), most instruments have conformed to the piano keyboard style. There are a few different sizes of keyboards. In this book, it is recommended to use a 32-key melodica. Basic student models are generally 32 keys, but there are a few companies that make a 37-key model with five additional higher keys, and Hammond makes a 44-key model with an input for amplification.

The melodica is used worldwide and fills a variety of musical roles. It can be used as a solo instrument performing melodica passages, and can just as easily be a harmonic instrument providing chords and background effects. The melodica is used as an introductory instrument to elementary school students in countries like Japan and Jamaica, and while often utilized as a beginner instrument, the melodica can also be found in the hands of experts and has made its way into many genres of music. Nat King Cole performed a melodica solo on national television in the 1960s. Augustus Pablo brought the melodica into the limelight back in the 1970s with his roots reggae and dub music. Brazilian composers (and living legends) Hermeto Pascoal and Jovino Santos Neto have used the melodica in their compositions and performances over the decades. John Batiste has been popularizing the melodica in recent years with his playing as band leader on "The Late Show with Steven Colbert," with exquisite improvisational skills and jazz chops. Viral videos of the professional group the Melodica Men have been circulating, showcasing the duo performing complicated classical pieces on melodica (seriously, check them out!). Melodica can also be found all over pop music from Steely Dan to Gorillaz and Oasis to Goldfrapp. The melodica is a unique instrument that can be played in many situations and brings joy to audiences and players alike.

YOUR MELODICA

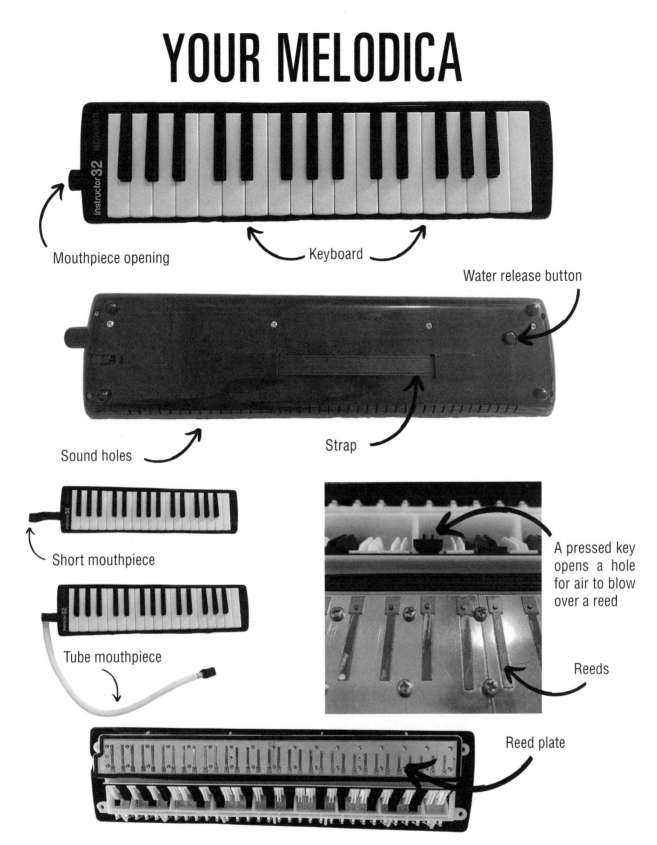

Mouthpiece opening

Keyboard

Water release button

Sound holes

Strap

Short mouthpiece

Tube mouthpiece

A pressed key opens a hole for air to blow over a reed

Reeds

Reed plate

Due to the nature of playing the melodica, a buildup of condensation can occur. There are three ways to remove condensation build-up/clean your instrument:

1. Quick Clean: Using the water release button. To quickly remove built-up condensation on the reed plate, push the water release button on the back of the instrument and blow through the mouthpiece without pressing any keys. Most melodicas come with a small cleaning cloth and that can also be used for a quick wipe and clean.

2. Disinfect: Mouthpieces should be cleaned and sanitized regularly. Rinse the short mouthpiece and/or tube mouthpiece with warm water, mix a solution of 50% water and 50% rubbing alcohol or hydrogen peroxide and submerge for 3-5 minutes. Rinse again with warm water and let air dry.

3. In Depth: Cleaning inside your melodica. To remove built-up condensation and sanitize the inside of your melodica, first unscrew and remove the plastic casing. Once the reed plate is exposed, use a cloth with a small amount of rubbing alcohol or hydrogen peroxide and gently swab over reeds, keys, and inside plastic casing.

FINGERING AND HAND POSITIONS

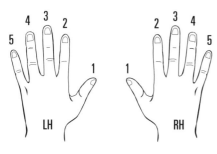

Finger numbers indicate where to place our hands on the keyboard for optimal technique and mobility. For all keyboard instruments, our fingers are numbered with thumb as 1, index as 2, middle as 3, ring as 4 and pinky as 5. RH stands for Right Hand and LH stands for Left Hand. This book will primarily only use RH.

Because our fingers are not all the same length, there are specific techniques to integrate into practice to make sure and maintain a healthy hand position. For example, when the thumb plays a key, you must move your arm forward to reach the key as opposed to "breaking" our wrist (see below) to get your thumb to reach.

Below are examples of healthy hand positions and unhealthy hand positions:

Curled fingers are an unhealthy hand position because you must force your fingers to be curled which causes unnecessary stress to the muscles and tendons in your hand.

You should not be playing with straight fingers either! This hinders mobility/agility and just like playing with curled fingers, puts unnecessary pressure on your hand.

A neutral and relaxed position is the healthiest hand position for melodica. Play on your fingertips, not the nails or the pads of your fingers.

PRO TIP:

Keeping your fingernails short helps to avoid nails clicking and sliding on the keyboard.

Nobody wants a broken wrist! When your wrist is "broken" as pictured, it puts undue pressure on the fingers, muscles, and tendons of the hands and wrists to do all the work, when really that is the **arm's** job. A healthy wrist is perfectly straight and not bending in any direction, so the arm can support the hand while it is playing the keys.

It's the same principle when typing on a computer, and why people use a wrist brace to keep the wrist from "breaking" while typing. Some people develop severe and painful injuries due to unhealthy habits and techniques in the music world, so make sure you are relaxed and aware each day you practice, so you can develop healthy habits!

Tabletop (on a table or in your lap) This position has your instrument either placed on a table or in your lap so you can use both hands. With this position, you must use the tube mouthpiece. This position is for beginner, intermediate, and expert players.

One-Handed with Tube In this position, you can be seated, standing, or mobile with the instrument while still being able to see the keyboard while playing. This position is for beginner, intermediate, and expert players. ***In this book we will be playing primarily in this position.***

One-Handed with Short Mouthpiece In this position you can be seated, standing, or mobile, but are unable to see the keyboard as you play. You may notice that it is easier to make a sound using the short mouthpiece and that is because when your breath is closer to the reeds, you need less air to make a sound. This position is for intermediate and expert players.

MOUTHPIECE TECHNIQUES

To make a sound on the melodica, there are two steps you must do simultaneously.

1. Blow air through the mouthpiece

2. Press a key (or multiple keys)

Because the melodica is a free reed instrument (like the harmonica or the accordion), if you only press down the keys, no sound will be made. The same is true if you only blow air through the mouthpiece: no sound will be made. You must do **both** at the same time to produce a sound. Most melodicas come with two different mouthpieces—the tube and the short mouthpiece—and there are slightly different ways to approach each one when playing.

Using the tube mouthpiece:

Hold the end of the tube mouthpiece lightly between your teeth (this prevents the mouthpiece from falling out of your mouth while playing) and press your lips tightly over the tip of the mouthpiece. Be sure your lips are sealed around the mouthpiece so that all your air is going directly into the instrument and not leaking out the side of your mouth.

Using the short mouthpiece:

Because this mouthpiece is stationary, there is no need to use your teeth at all. Simply wrap your lips around the tip of the mouthpiece like you are drinking out of a straw. Be sure your lips are sealed around the mouthpiece, so that all your air is going directly into the instrument and not leaking out the side of your mouth.

ARTICULATION

There are two ways to approach articulating sounds on the melodica. One is the **finger method**, using your fingers to produce specific sounds (i.e., short, long, punctuated, etc.) and the other is the **tonguing method**, using air and mouth articulation to produce specific sounds. Most melodica playing is a combination of both, because you must use your fingers and your mouth to play the instrument, but there are times when one or the other is most appropriate. In both cases, taking big deep breaths using your diaphragm is key to proper breathing and breath control.

When using the **finger method**, you will blow a steady stream of air through your mouthpiece and let your fingers do the work playing rhythms. To try this, put any RH finger on any key. While breathing steadily, hit the key four times.

When using the **tonguing method**, you will articulate each note and rhythm with your air and mouth by allowing a specific amount of air to pass through the mouthpiece. To do this, pretend you are saying the word "do" through your mouthpiece. (Don't actually say the word, just mouth it.) To try this, put any RH finger on any key. Keep the key pressed down and mouth the word "do" four times.

The above examples should sound very similar but feel fairly different. Try using both methods with the song below.

RHYTHMS

There are three basic elements that make up music: rhythm, melody, and harmony. **Rhythm** tells us how long to hold a note or rest. To play any rhythm properly, you must begin with a *steady beat*. A steady beat keeps the song at a steady speed and if you were to tap your foot along with a song, that would be the steady beat. For instance, think of the ABC song and before singing it count "1-2-3-4 ~ A-B-C-D...." Counting "1-2-3-4" before you sing sets you up with a steady beat so when you sing the song, it's all the same speed. Below are three basic rhythms to get us started:

Let's Play! 🔊

Using your RH, place fingers 2 and 3 on a set of two black keys. Finger numbers are always written above the notes. To feel a steady beat before you start, count "1-2-3-4."

TWO BLACK KEYS

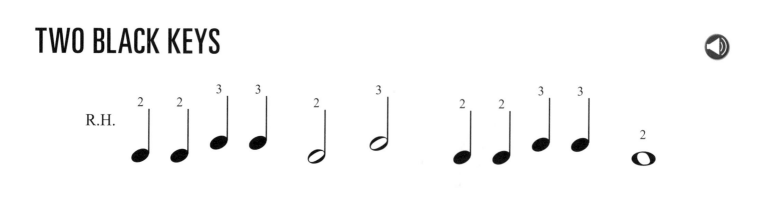

NOTES ON THE MELODICA

lower ⟵——————⟶ higher

The musical alphabet consists of seven notes (ABCDEFG) and is the foundation for playing music on the melodica and any other instrument with a keyboard. The keyboard is made of a particular pattern of white and black keys and the musical alphabet is repeated from left to right. The lower tones start on the left and get higher as you play to the right. Above is the musical alphabet on a 32-key melodica.

The pattern of groups of two and three black keys makes it easy to identify which note is which on the white keys. For example, the note D is always located between a set of two black keys. Try finding all the D's on the melodica from low to high, followed by all the A's, B's and so on.

Let's Play!

When reading music, you will read the same way you would read a book: from left to right, and then down to the next line. Additionally, music is divided into equal sections called **measures** or **bars** and separated by **bar lines**. A **final bar line** is used to signal the end of the song. You may notice that this song has four beats per measure.

THE C-D-E SONG

This song uses all three rhythms we have learned. Make sure to count a steady "1-2-3-4" before you start to feel a beat and set the **tempo** (or speed) of the song.

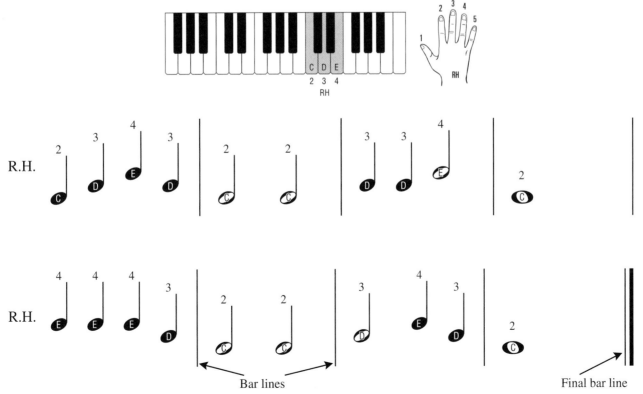

Bar lines

Final bar line

MUSICAL SYMBOLS AND NOTES ON THE STAFF

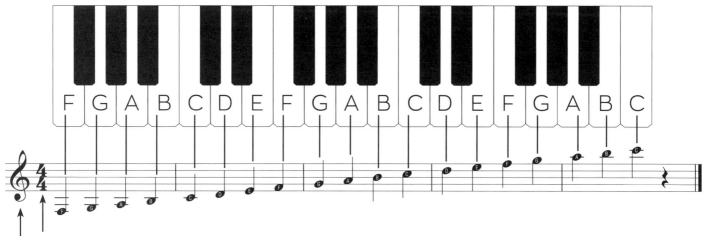

Time Signature: The top number tells us how many beats are in each measure and the bottom number tells us the quarter note gets one beat.

Treble Clef and Staff: Music is written on the staff (five lines with four spaces in between, shown above) to determine which note should be played. Each note on the melodica has its own special place on the staff as shown. The treble clef is the fancy looking symbol to the left of the time signature signaling the notes are in a higher register. Melodica music is written in treble clef.

♩	Quarter note	𝄽	Quarter rest	1 beat
♪	Half note	▬	Half rest	2 beats
𝅗𝅥	Whole note	▬	Whole rest	4 beats

Notes and Rests: Each of the rhythms we learned on page 8 has a corresponding **rest** that gets the same number of beats. A rest sign tells us when and how long to NOT play in music giving us beats of silence. For example, if the quarter note tells us to hold a key for one beat, a quarter rest tells us make no sound for one beat.

Measures: Music is divided into equal sections called measures or bars. Each measure contains the same number of beats throughout the song and the top number of the time signature tells us how many beats are in each measure. Measures are sectioned off by bar lines and there is always a final bar line at the end of the song signaling the player to stop.

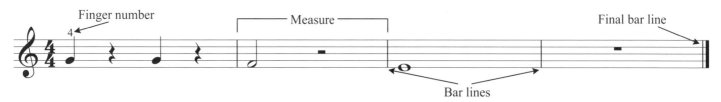

Stems on the Notes: You may notice that notes with stems (quarter notes and half notes) will sometimes have stems going up and sometimes have stems going down. The direction of the stem has no effect on the note at all. Notes on the middle line of the staff or higher point down, and notes below the middle line point up.

THE KEY OF C

The key of C is based off the C major scale, which is a series of seven notes. Below are the notes in a C major scale. Above the staff are finger numbers to help play the scale smoothly. You may recognize the sound as Do-Re-Mi-Fa-Sol-La-Ti-Do and that is correct! The notes in a major scale are the same as Do-Re-Mi-Fa-Sol-La-Ti-Do.

C MAJOR SCALE

The fingering for the C major scale has the 1 tucking under the 3 on the way up, and the 3 crossing over the 1 on the way down. Remember to keep a straight wrist when using this fingering!

Let's Play!

HOT DOG BUNS

In some music, there will be **breath marks** indicated above the staff to help guide your breathing while you play. Breath marks look like a big comma sign. Notice the breath marks in this tune!

MARY HAD A LITTLE LAMB

DYNAMICS

Dynamic symbols in music tell us how loudly or softly to play. Dynamics on the melodica are created by the breath. The more air you use, the louder the sound and the less air you use, the quieter the sound. Our fundamental dynamic symbols are:

Dynamic symbol:	*pp*	*p*	*mp*	*mf*	*f*	*ff*
Name (Italian):	*pianissimo*	*piano*	*mezzo piano*	*mezzo forte*	*forte*	*fortissimo*
Meaning:	very soft	soft	moderately soft	moderately loud	loud	very loud

crescendo or cresc.
getting gradually louder

diminuendo or dim. or decrescendo
getting gradually softer

Let's Play!

Watch out for the finger change in measure 7!

ARE YOU SLEEPING?

Keeping a steady beat while playing music is essential and different songs have different tempos (or speeds). To make sure you are playing the correct tempo, set a metronome to the indicated BPM (beats per minute). Below, "Ode to Joy" has a quarter note equaling 90 BPM. To play along with the track, you will need to set your metronome to 90 BPM.

ODE TO JOY

PRO TIP:

If you're just starting out a song, you may not be able to play as fast as the BPM indicates. Don't worry! You can always start slower and work your way up to the indicated speed. Practice makes progress!

INTERVALS

An interval is the distance between two notes. For example, the interval of F to G is called a 2nd and the interval of F to A is called a 3rd (shown below). The bigger the interval, the further the distance between the two notes.

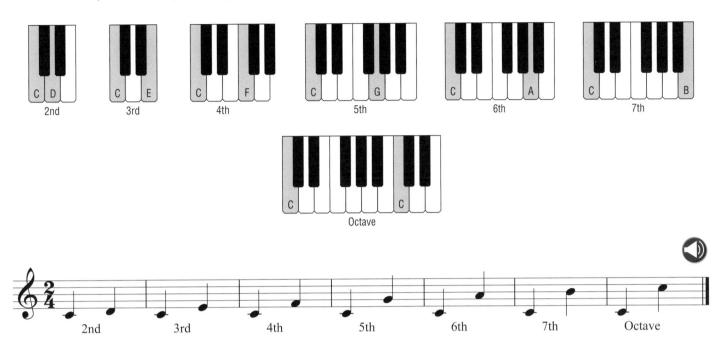

The way each interval looks on the staff is different. As shown above, an interval of a 2nd is always going from a line to the very next space or a space to the very next line. 3rds are always going from a line to the very next line or a space to the very next space. For larger intervals, the pattern is continued. Intervals are the foundation to creating one of the most important elements in music: **melody**. Melody is an essential component to most music and is played one note at a time and is heard as the main theme and/or what you would sing along to. All the songs in this book up to page 27 are **melodies**.

Let's Play!

Be on the lookout for 2nds, 3rds, and 5ths in this song!

GO TELL AUNT RHODY IN MAJOR AND MINOR

HALF-STEPS, SHARPS, FLATS, AND NATURALS

A half-step is a specific interval that goes from one key to the VERY next key without skipping over any keys. Sharps and flats (accidentals) are two symbols in music that indicate to move either a half-step higher or lower. A sharp (#) tells us to go a half-step higher and a flat (♭) tells us to go a half-step lower.

Sharp and flat symbols apply to all repeating notes within the measure after the symbol appears. When a new measure begins, the symbols no longer apply, and the sharp or flat must be written in again.

A natural symbol (♮) cancels out a sharp or flat and means to play the natural note instead. Just like with the sharp and flat symbols, this will apply to any repeated note within the measure after the symbol occurs.

Let's Play!

This piece has repeated sections and a special ending. When you see a repeat sign, that means to go back to the nearest **backwards repeat sign** and repeat that section. If there are no backwards repeat signs, then simply go back to the beginning and play the whole song again. There are three repeated sections in this song. At the end, you will notice the new symbols: these are called 1st and 2nd endings. When you play the last section the first time, you take ending 1. When you play the last section the second time, you will skip over ending 1 and take ending 2.

IN THE HALL OF THE MOUNTAIN KING

THE KEY OF G

The key of G is based off the G major scale. Every major scale is comprised of seven notes in a specific pattern of half-steps and whole steps. We learned about half steps on the previous page (one key to the very next key) and a whole step is two half-steps put together. On the keyboard, a whole step has one key in between. For example, a C to a D would be a whole step with the C# in between, or an E to an F# would be a whole step with the F in between. Below is the G major scale notes and our major scale pattern with finger numbers above. The key signature is shown at the beginning of the treble staff and indicates how many sharps or flats are in the key. The key of C has no sharps or flats, and the key of G has one sharp (F#).

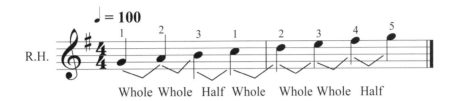

Let's Play!

LIGHTLY ROW

KEY SIGNATURES AND TRANSPOSING

Every major scale must contain the entire musical alphabet in order and use the whole step/half-step pattern. That means you can't skip over a letter in the alphabet, and you can't double up on a letter in the alphabet. Because of this rule, there are only sharp key signatures or flat key signatures; there will never be a key signature that has both sharps and flats. The only exception to this rule is the Key of C which has no sharps or flats. For example, the key of G's major scale is:

Even though an F# and a Gb are technically the same note, we must call the 7th note in a G major scale an F# because of the alphabet rule. **Transposing** is when you play the exact same intervals and rhythms of a song in a different key. Let's try a C major scale exercise, then transpose to the key of G. Remember when you switch to the key of G, the first note is G and all F's are F#!

TRANSPOSITION MISSION

PRO CHALLENGE:

Try transposing the songs we played in the key of C from pages 11 and 12 to the key of G. Here are the first notes of each song to get you started: "Hot Dog Buns," "Mary Had a Little Lamb,"and "Ode to Joy" will begin on B, and "Are You Sleeping" will begin on G.

Now try transposing "Lightly Row" on page 15 to C. It will begin on G.

LEGATO AND STACCATO

Legato is a term in music that means to play each note smoothly into the next note without any breaks in sound. If there are no markings to indicate otherwise, legato playing is the default way to play. However, there are markings that tell us when to specifically play legato called slurs (or phrase marks) that look like this:

PRO TIP:

If no breath marks are indicated, the end of a phrase is the perfect time to take a breath.

Staccato notes are to be played short and separated from neighboring notes, and are shown in music with a dot on top of or below the note (depending on the direction of the stem) like this:

Let's Play!
In the last measure, two notes playing at the same time create **harmony**.

ARE YOU SCARY?

PRO TIP:

When you see a staccato note, you should use the tonguing method to keep your note short and articulated.

Let's Play!

SURPRISE SYMPHONY

EIGHTH NOTES

Eighth notes are rhythms in music that get a half beat each. To accommodate half beats, we say "and" after each number count. For example, instead of counting "1-2-3-4" at the beginning of a song to establish a steady beat, try counting "1 and 2 and 3 and 4 and" to get the feel for eighth note rhythms.

Eighth notes can appear a few different ways. One eighth note by itself looks like this: ♪ or ♪

Two eighth notes together have a beam that connects them, and they look like this: ♫ or ♫

And if there are four eighth notes grouped together, they can also have a beam across all four and they look like this: ♫♫ or ♫♫

Let's Play!

SKIP TO MY LOU

PICK-UPS AND INCOMPLETE MEASURES

Sometimes a song can start with pick-up notes or an incomplete measure. You can identify this right away, because the first measure will not match the time signature. For example, if the **time signature** is 4/4 (remember, the top number tells us how many beats are supposed to be in each measure) and the first measure only has two beats in it, you will count "1-2-3-4-1-2" and begin the song on beat 3. Often, the missing beats are made up at the end of a song, but that's not always the case. Pick-ups and incomplete measures exist as a way to keep correct timing within songs and produce interesting phrasing within the music.

Let's Play!

BABY BUMBLEBEE

DOTTED RHYTHMS

When there is a dot next to a note, that means to add half the note's value to the note. For example, a half note = 2 beats. Half of 2 = 1.

Add 2 + 1 and you have the value of a dotted half note = 3.

$\textstyle\unicode{x1D15E} + \cdot = \unicode{x1D15E}\cdot$
2 + 1 = 3

Let's Play!

This song has a new time signature. The top number (3) indicates how many beats are in each measure and the bottom number (4) still indicates that the quarter note gets the beat. We will have to establish our tempo a bit differently to accommodate one fewer beat by counting "1-2-3" before we start.

ROW, ROW, ROW YOUR BOAT

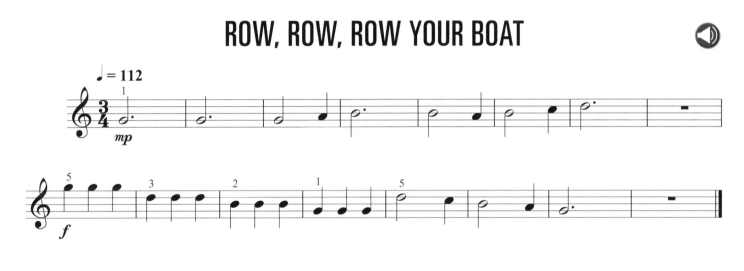

When there is a dot next to a quarter note, we use the same formula as above to figure out how long to hold it for: A quarter note = 1 beat. Half of 1 = ½. Add 1 + ½ and you get the value of a dotted quarter note = 1½ $\quad \unicode{x2669} + \cdot = \unicode{x2669}\cdot$
1 + ½ = 1½

Let's Play!

ALOUETTE

TIED NOTES

Tied notes connect two or more rhythms of the same pitch together adding the values of each rhythm. The tied notes will be played as one note but counted with each of the notes' values. For example, if we tied together a whole note on an F and a quarter note on the same F, we would hold it for a total of five beats. A tie looks like a curved line connecting the heads of notes together (see below). Tied notes can be used to create specific phrasing, to elongate notes within a song or to simply add interesting rhythms in a piece of music.

PRO TIP:

Ties and slurs look almost identical. The way to easily tell them apart is that tied notes are ALWAYS the exact same note on the staff and slurs always phrase together different notes that are meant to be played legato.

Let's Play!

LIMEHOUSE BLUES

Let's Play!

Putting it all together: this tune has a pick-up note, dotted-half notes, eighth notes, ties, and it has a 3/4 time signature.

MY BONNIE LIES OVER THE OCEAN

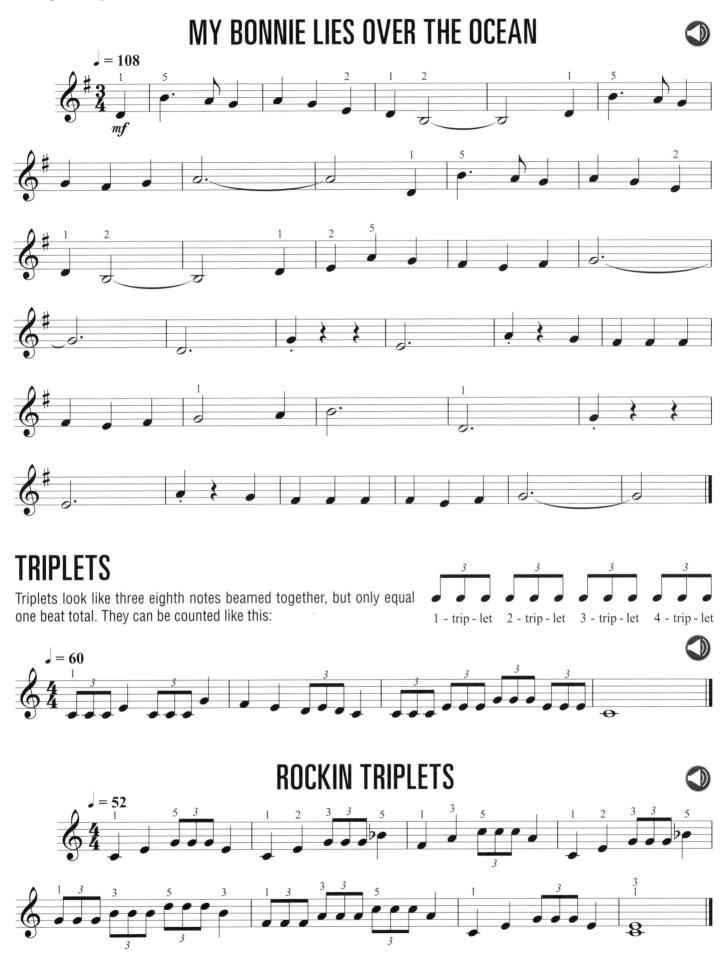

TRIPLETS

Triplets look like three eighth notes beamed together, but only equal one beat total. They can be counted like this:

1 - trip - let   2 - trip - let   3 - trip - let   4 - trip - let

ROCKIN TRIPLETS

SWING RHYTHM

Many styles of music feel eighth note rhythms as a **swing rhythm**. Swing rhythm (or swing feel) can be indicated by the music simply stating, "swing feel" or "swing rhythm" and/or by showing one of the following symbols:

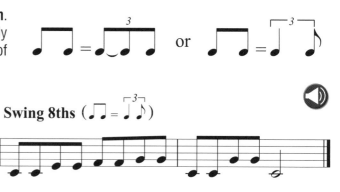

PRO TIP:

A great way to visualize the difference between straight eighth notes and swing eighth notes is to imagine walking fast on straight eighth notes and skipping on swing eighth notes.

FERMATA

You will notice a new symbol (⌒) in this tune at measure 6. This is called a **fermata**, and when you see this symbol over a note or rest, it means to hold it longer than the value of the note or rest.

HAPPY BIRTHDAY

PRO CHALLENGE:

Can you go back to page 18 and 19 and play "Baby Bumblebee" and "Alouette" with a swing rhythm?

KEY OF F

The key of F is based off the F major scale. Just like every key, the key of F is comprised of seven notes in a specific pattern of whole steps and half steps. Below are the F major scale notes with finger numbers above. Our key signature is shown at the beginning of the treble staff. You will notice that in the key of F has one flat: B♭.

Let's Play!

TWINKLE, TWINKLE LITTLE STAR

CHOUCOUNE

PRO CHALLENGE:

Can you transpose all the songs from pages 11 and 12 to the key of F? "Hot Dog Buns," "Mary Had a Little Lamb," and "Ode to Joy" will begin on A, and "Are You Sleeping" will begin on F.

CHROMATIC SCALE

The chromatic scale (or playing "chromatically") is based solely on half steps. For example, the chromatic scale starting on a C would hit every single note (all black keys and white keys) without skipping over any keys until it reached the next C on the keyboard, as shown below.

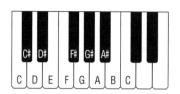

Let's Play!

ENTRY OF THE GLADIATORS

Putting in all together—let's try this famous Scott Joplin tune that includes many of the topics covered up to this point. One of the most prominent ragtime composers of all time, Mr. Joplin was crucial to the development of this African American-born genre that influenced other musical genres such as stride piano and early jazz.

THE ENTERTAINER

CHORDS (AND HOW TO READ THEM)

A **chord** is three or more notes played together to form **harmony** within the key. Harmony (one of the three basic elements in music) is used to complement and support the **melody.** Melody is the main musical theme in music.

TRIADS

Triads are basic chords that get their name because of how many notes are in them: three. These three-note chords consist of three parts: the root, the 3rd, and the 5th. We will start by playing these triads in **root position** which means the root is the lowest note, the 3rd is the middle note, and the 5th is the highest note. You will notice that **root position triads** are stacked in thirds. It is also important to know that the root names the chord. For example, if you play C-E-G all at the same time, you have a C chord. If you play F-A-C all at the same time, you have an F chord.

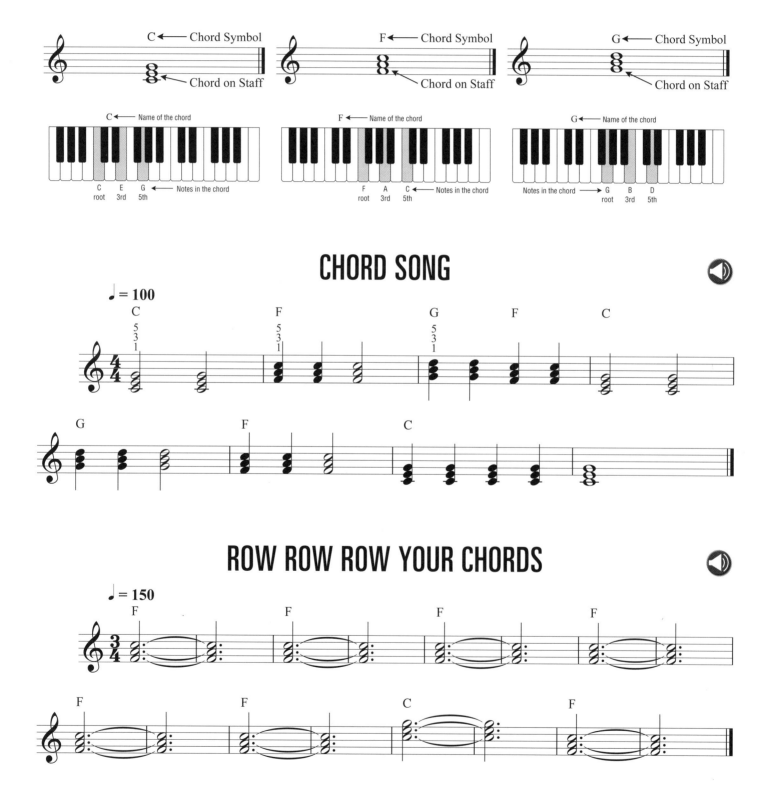

CHORD SONG

ROW ROW ROW YOUR CHORDS

Let's Play!

The songs on the previous page show the two different ways to read chords: reading each note on the staff and reading chord symbols above the staff. Chord symbols are an alternative to writing music on the staff and are often written above the staff on sheet music. Chord symbols can sometimes be used instead of sheet music when playing with a rock, blues, pop, country, or jazz band. Let's try playing a song using only chords symbols with a whole note as our rhythm.

HUSH LITTLE BABY

CHORDIALLY

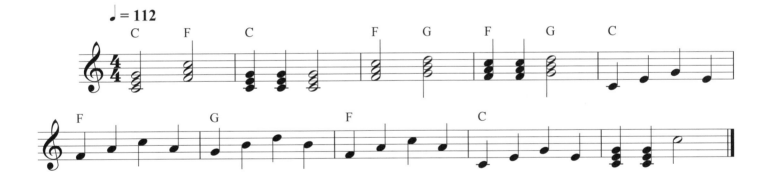

MAJOR AND MINOR CHORDS

The two* primary types of triads are major and minor. A major triad has a major 3rd between the root and 3rd. A minor chord has a minor 3rd between the root and 3rd.

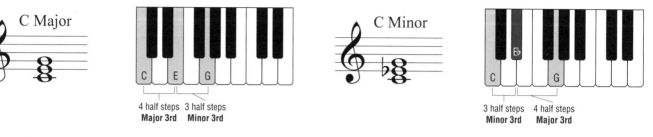

C Major

4 half steps 3 half steps
Major 3rd **Minor 3rd**

C Minor

3 half steps 4 half steps
Minor 3rd **Major 3rd**

*Because triads are built on two intervals of 3rds put together, and there are two different types of 3rds, there are four types of triads (major, minor, diminished and augmented). Flip to the chord chart on the back page to learn more about all the different types of chords! If we play the C major scale all in triads starting on C, our chord progression will look like this:

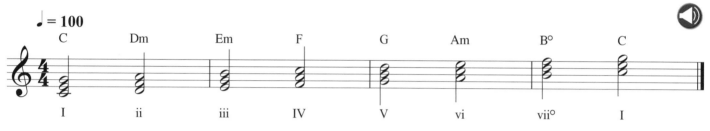

♩ = 100

C   Dm   Em   F   G   Am   B°   C

I   ii   iii   IV   V   vi   vii°   I

The Roman numerals under each chord represent the placement of each within the key. Since C is the first note of the scale, C chord will be the I chord. Since D is the second note of the scale, Dm will be the ii chord, and so on.

PRO TIP:

When playing multiple notes on the melodica (like chords!), the air is distributed between multiple reeds, forcing the player to use more air. Because more air is needed to play chords, make sure you're getting a deep breath!

Let's Play!

Now, let's try a song using some major and minor chords:

MOLLY MALONE

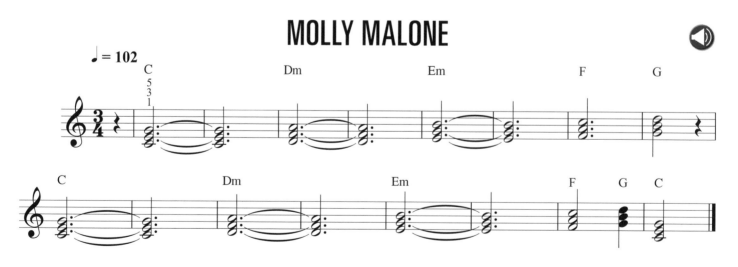

♩ = 102

C   Dm   Em   F   G

C   Dm   Em   F   G   C

PRO CHALLENGE:

The melody for "Molly Malone" has a separate audio track. Can you play the chords to "Molly Malone" with the melody track?

INVERSIONS

Inversions are chords that use the same notes as root position chords (where the root is the lowest note), but inverted so that the 3rd or the 5th is the lowest note. Inversions are often used as "shortcuts" to other chords, making the transition between chords smooth and sonically pleasing.

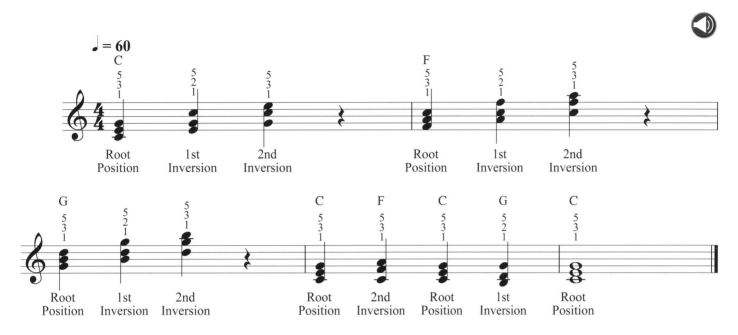

Let's Play!

AMAZING GRACE

PRO CHALLENGE:

The melody for "Amazing Grace" has a separate audio track. Can you play the chords to "Amazing Grace" with the melody track?

TRIAD VOCAB

Since all triads are made up of 3rds, its helpful to learn "Triad Vocab." Memorizing these seven different three-note patterns can also help in identifying triads that are not in root position. Here are our seven triad groups:

A-C-E

B-D-F

C-E-G

D-A-F

E-G-B

F-A-C

G-B-D

This works for all four different types of triads (major, minor, diminished, and augmented). Simply add sharps or flats as needed. For example, an F minor chord would be F-A♭-C. The three basic letter names are still the same, but lowering the middle note a half-step makes it F minor. For an E major triad, we'd make the G a G♯.

While root position, first, and second inversion chords are quite useful and played constantly in music, there are even more ways to play chords than these three ways! For example, any combination or order of C-E-G will always be a C major triad, because those are the specific note combinations that make up that specific chord. This is another reason to memorize the "Triad Vocab" so you can readily identify chords even when they are in disguise.

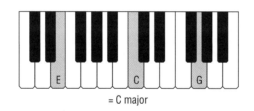

= C major

BIGGER CHORDS

Beyond triads, there are *many* different types of four-note chords (and beyond). We are going to stick to a few of the basic four-note chords in this section, starting with the most popular: 7th chords. A 7th chord is when you add a 7th on top of your root, 3rd, and 5th.

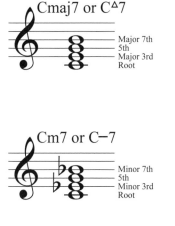

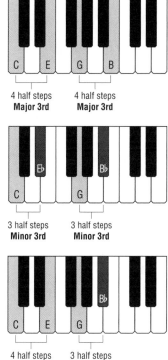

The root of a chord is always stable and names the chord. With these particular chords, the 5th is also stable and does not change (however, sometimes 5ths can be flat or sharp and will be indicated by a #5 or ♭5). It's the 3rds and 7ths that generally determine the harmonic quality of the chord. And just as 3rds can be major or minor, so can 7ths.

7th chords add much more color and excitement to music, giving the listener and the player alike a broader appreciation of the richness in sound. These types of chords are found in all types of music and all three of these four-note chord examples occur naturally in every major scale.

Let's Play!

7THS SONG

PRO CHALLENGE:

Can you play this song with a swing rhythm?

Some of the most recognizable holiday songs come from the "Nutcracker Suite" composed by Pyotr Ilyich Tchaikovsky in 1892. This is a collection of eight songs to accompany the well-known ballet. Tchaikovsky also composed music for the ballets "The Sleeping Beauty" and "Swan Lake."

NUTCRACKER: MARCH

CHORD GROUPS

Every key has groups of chords that are used frequently together to form harmony in music. When these chord groups are put together in a song, they are called "chord progressions." One of the most recognizable chord progressions is called the I-IV-V and is based on the 1st, 4th, and 5th degrees (or notes) of the major scale.

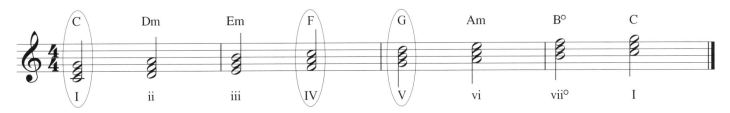

Often, a 7th is added to the V chord and the progression looks like this: I-IV-V7. Adding the 7th to the V chord creates extra tension to that chord to lead it back to the I chord. If you take notice, you will find that almost every song will end on the I chord because that gives a sense of resolution. A fundamental element in music is the balance between tension and resolution within chords and melodies. The V chord gives tension, and its purpose is to lead us back to resolution (often the I chord). Below are inversions and shortcut ways to get to the IV and V7 chords quickly and easily from the root position I chord.

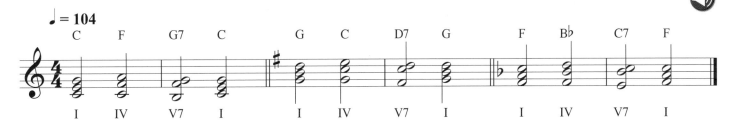

Let's Play!

First, play the chords to this song (written above the staff) and use the inversions shown above for the key of C. Play using a whole note rhythm to start, and once you get the hang of the chords, you may try other rhythms. After you've practiced the chords, try playing the melody. The last two measures of the melody are missing! Can you find notes that match the chord and finish the song?

ROCKIN' CHORDS

"Lavender's Blue" is separated into two parts: chords and melody. The chords are written out in a particular way that has the player hitting the lowest note of the chord alone one time, then hitting the other two notes in the chord together two times. This is a very common way to play broken chords in 3/4 time. Practice the chords to "Lavender's Blue" first, and when you are ready, play along with the melody in the audio. Then switch to practicing the melody. When you're comfortable, go ahead and play along with the chords.

LAVENDER'S BLUE CHORDS

LAVENDER'S BLUE MELODY

The 12-bar blues is a 12-measure chord progression that uses the chords I-IV-V, and often turns each chord into a dominant 7th. Below are all the root position dominant 7th chords in a 12-bar blues progression.

12-BAR BLUES

KEY OF D

The key of D is based off the D major scale. Just like every key, the key of D is comprised of seven notes in a specific pattern of whole steps and half steps. Below are the D major scale notes with RH finger numbers above and scale degrees (Roman numerals) below. Our key signature is shown at the beginning of the treble staff. Please note that the key of D has two sharps: F♯ and C♯.

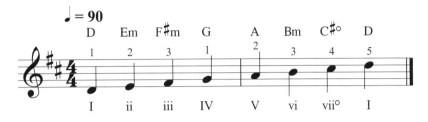

Let's Play!

This song's original key is G (in fact, its full title is Minuet in G) and you may recognize this famous melody. We've transposed it to D below to get practice playing in the key of D.

MINUET (IN D)

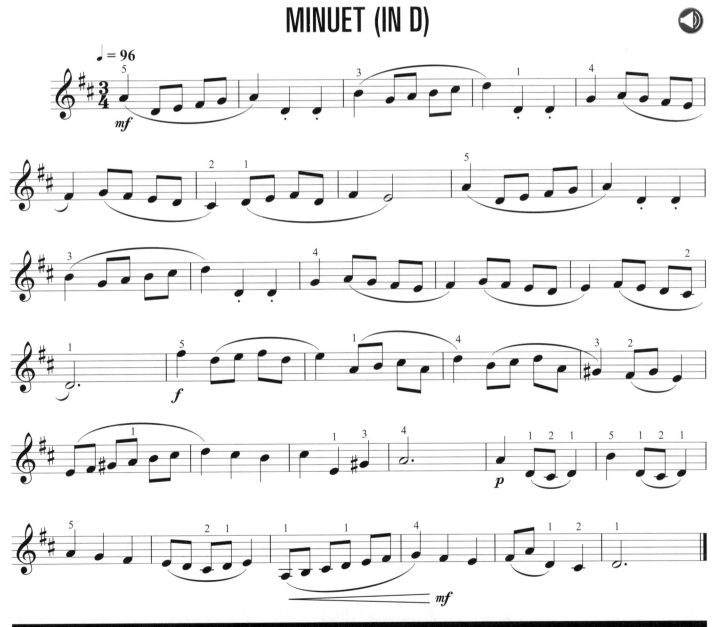

PRO CHALLENGE:

Can you transpose "Lightly Row" from page 15 to the key of D? The first note will be A.

ARPEGGIOS

Arpeggios, sometimes called broken chords, are chord notes that are played one at a time.

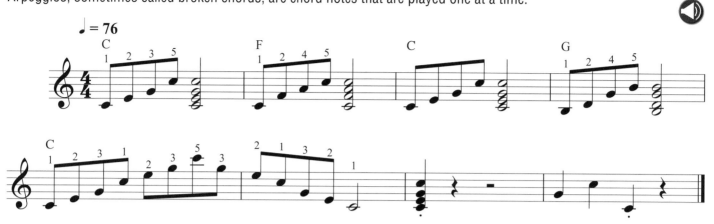

Arpeggios still function as **harmony** within a song, but with this next song "Bugle Call" you will notice that the entire song's melody is made up of one broken chord. Can you name the chord?

BUGLE CALL

SCARBOROUGH FAIR

PRO CHALLENGE:

The melody for "Scarborough Fair" has a separate audio track. Can you play the chords to "Scarborough Fair" with the melody track?

This is one of the world's most popular songs and it contains a chord progression you might recognize. Johann Pachelbel (1653-1706) was a German composer who wrote over 500 songs in his lifetime. You will see that Pachelbel uses a repetitive chord progression and sometimes includes arpeggios in the melody.

You may notice in the second last measure there is an abbreviated word: *rit.* This stands for the Italian word *ritardando* and it means to gradually slow down.

PACHEBEL'S CANON IN D

PRO CHALLENGE:

Can you compose your own melody using the same chords? Hint: using chord tones (or notes in the chord) is a good place to start!

KEY OF A

The key of A is based off the A major scale. Below are the A major scale notes with RH finger numbers above and scale degrees (Roman numerals) below. Our key signature is shown at the beginning of the staff. Please note that the key of A has three sharps: F#, C#, and G#.

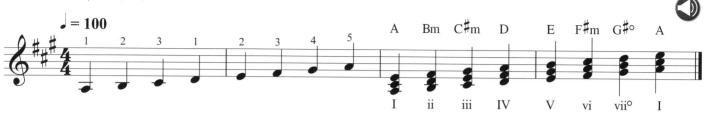

Let's Play!

There is a key signature change in this song and is indicated at the double bar line at the end of measure 16. While our song starts in the key of A, it switches to the key of D mid-song. There is also a new symbol in this tune called an accent when you see this symbol it means to add emphasis or stress this note making it louder and more prominent. You can do this using a stronger force of breath.

CAN CAN

THE BLUES SCALE

The **blues scale** is a six-note scale used in blues and jazz music. Below are the notes in the C blues scale with two different options for fingering. Use the fingering that feels the most comfortable to your hand.

Let's Play!

The blues chord progression is a 12-measure form using the I IV V7 chord groups. Below is a C blues scale exercise over a 12-bar blues:

PLAY ALONG BLUES

PRO CHALLENGE:

There are two audio tracks for "Play Along Blues": the melody version and the chords version. Can you play the melody with the chord track and vice versa?

DID YOU KNOW?

In addition to being a popular 12-measure chord progression, the **blues** is also an American roots genre of music. This African American art form derived from a mix of spirituals, work songs, and the blending of African and European influences in the American South in the late 19th century. Still widely popular today, the blues is responsible for sparking other American music genres such as jazz, R&B, Rock 'n' Roll and Country.

Let's Play!

The tune below has two treble clef staffs joined together and requires reading both lines simultaneously, using the RH and the LH. To play this song, you will need to be in the "tabletop" or "in your lap" position and use the long mouthpiece.

TWO-HAND BLUES

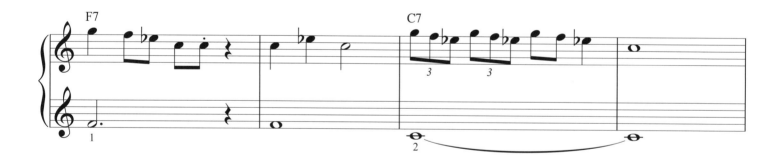

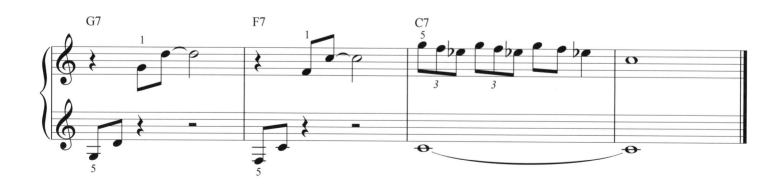

IMPROVISING

Blues music is popular for many reasons. First, it has a basic chord structure, making it easy for beginners and experts alike to play. It's also an exceedingly expressive art form, allowing vocalists to sing about their emotions. Instrumentalists are often granted improvised solos to express musically how they feel in the moment. To **improvise** means to compose on the spot. When players improvise, that means they are not reading music! They are using their ear, musical tools, and knowledge from studying and practicing, to create melodies and express themselves.

Using the notes in a C blues scale, improvise the missing melody notes within this 12-bar blues.

MISSING MELODY

PRO CHALLENGE:

Can you improvise over the entire song?

In addition to using the blues scale as inspiration for improvised melodies, another tool we can use is chord tones (notes within a chord). For this exercise, try using chord tones as well as notes in the blues scales to create the missing melodies.

MYSTERY MELODY

MORE KEY SIGNATURES

The Key of E

Let's Play!

OH WHEN THE SAINTS GO MARCHING IN

The Key of B

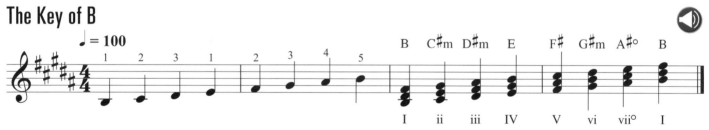

Let's Play!

KUMBAYA

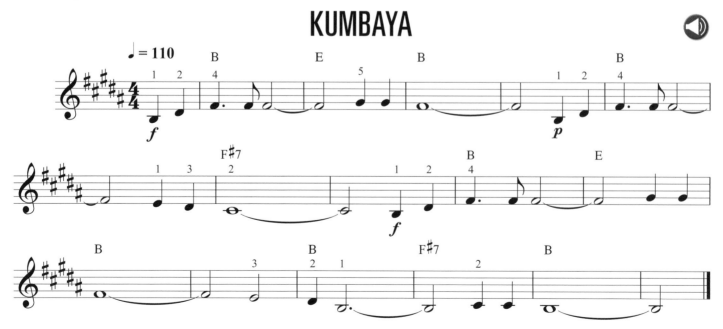

The Key of F#

You may notice that there are six sharps in this key including a white key sharp: E#. Even though E# and F are technically the same note, we must call it E# in this key because of the alphabet rule.

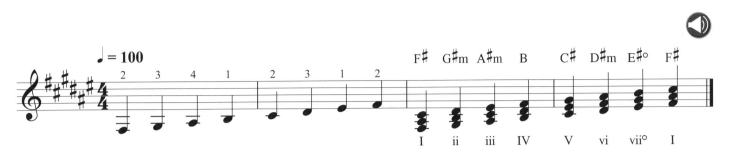

Let's Play!

LULLABY

The Key of D♭

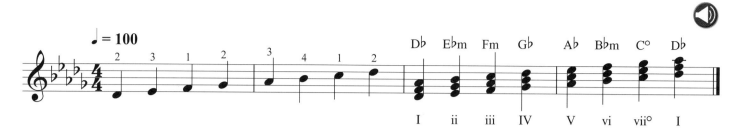

Let's Play!

POP GOES THE WEASEL

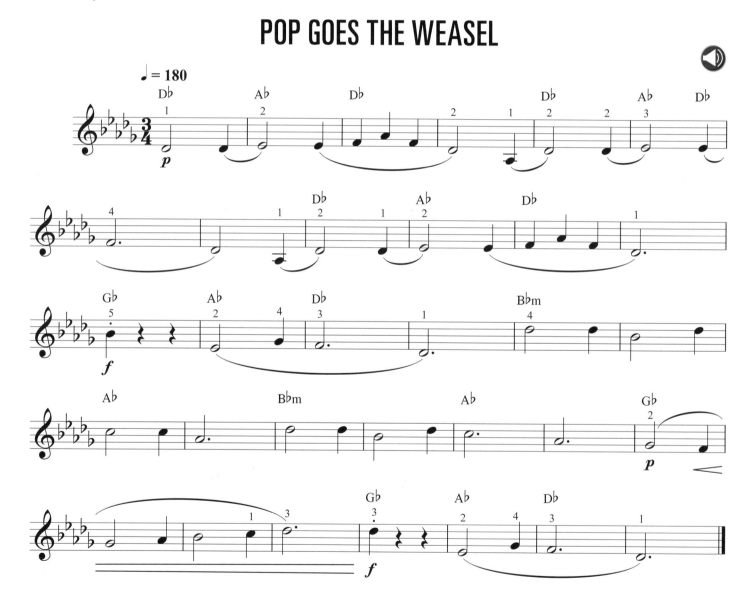

The Key of A♭

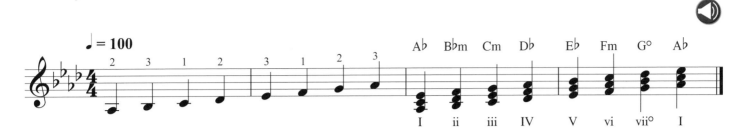

Let's Play!

YANKEE DOODLE

The Key of E♭

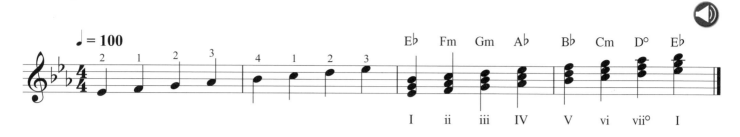

Let's Play!

AURA LEE

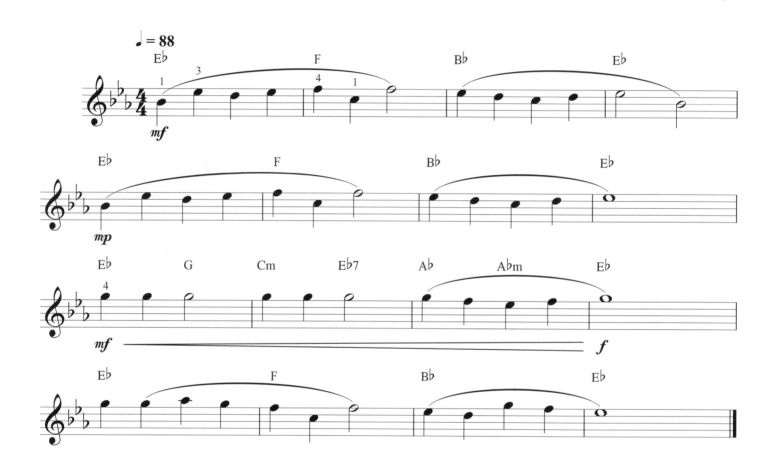

The Key of B♭

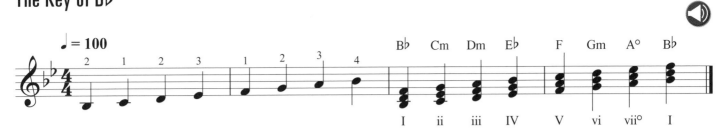

Let's Play!

OH DANNY BOY

PRO CHALLENGE:

Can you play all the songs from the More Key Signatures section in all 12 keys?

VIBRATO

A distinct sound you can create using your breath on the melodica is **vibrato**. Vibrato occurs when you rapidly change the speed of your breath while playing a note to produce a pitch that sounds as if it's wavering or vibrating. Violinists and other stringed instrumentalists use vibrato in their playing by rapidly moving the finger that is pushing the string to produce the same effect, and you will often hear singers (especially opera singers) use vibrato with their voice. Vibrato gives music depth and can create an emotional soundscape.

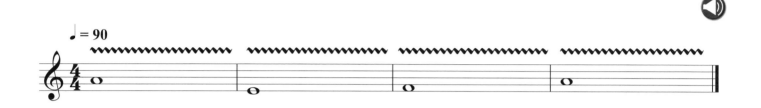

You will notice there are many different types of chords in this tune, including augmented chords which have a + sign next to them. That means to raise the 5th up a half-step (#5).

MY MELANCHOLY BABY

Franz Schubert was an Austrian composer who wrote over 600 songs. Considering he only lived to be 31 years old, his extensive body of work is quite impressive, ranging from full operas and symphonies to string quartets and piano sonatas. "Ave Maria" is one of the world's most popular songs, with a very moving chord progression.

AVE MARIA

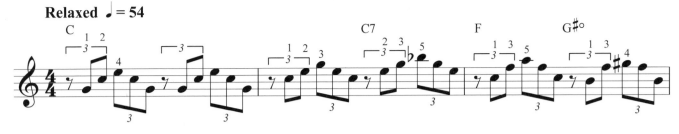

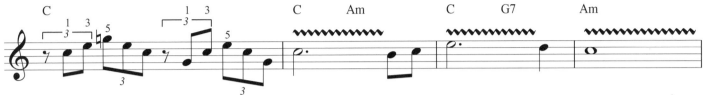

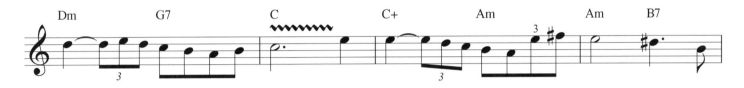

TRILLS

Rapidly going back and forth between two neighboring notes is called a **trill**, and it can create an exciting fluttering effect on the keyboard. Trills are often found in classical music, but they are also found in many other styles.

PEG O' MY HEART

PRO TIP:

Trill and vibrato markings look exactly the same....EXCEPT a trill marking will always have the letters "tr" in front of the marking. Notice the marking over the last note of the song above: is it a trill or vibrato?

Still viewed as one of the most influential composers of all time, Wolfgang Amadeus Mozart was considered a genius during his life as a musician and composer from 1756-1791. After composing his first songs at age 5, Mozart went on to write nearly 800 works, from solo piano to complete operas and many genres in between. A multi-instrumentalist and true go-getter of his time, Mozart's music is still being performed all over the world.

RONDO ALLA TURCA

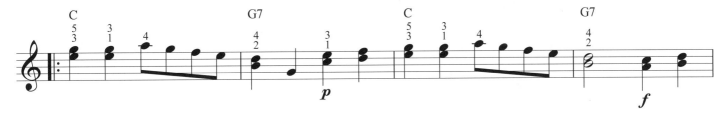

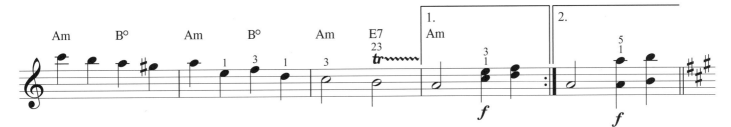

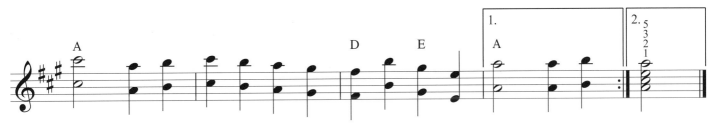

ROLLS

Rolls are a series of notes played very quickly. The rapidity is similar to trills, but often rolled notes or chords use many different notes as opposed to only two. These are the two types of rolls we will use in this book:

1. **Rolled chords**. This is a broken or arpeggiated chord played very fast. This creates a unique sound and is a fun way to add something special to your music. A roll is notated by a vertical wavy line to the left of the chord that is meant to be rolled (see example below).

2. **Melody rolls**. This technique has the player rolling up or down melodically with notes leading to the main melody note. Often these are half notes, but that is not always the case. These rolls are also meant to be played very fast and are notated by miniature-looking notes called grace notes (see example below). Melodic rolls can be a great tool for improvising cool sounds in jazz and blues and can be played even when they are not notated.

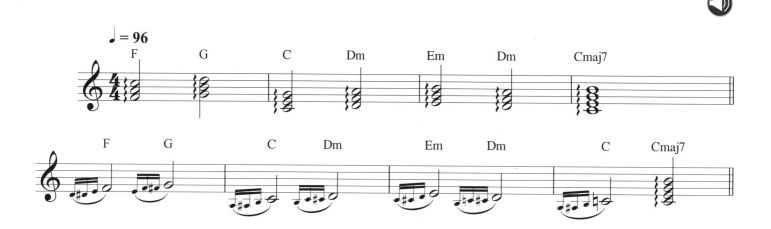

It is important to distinguish grace notes from actual eighth notes as the rhythm and melody will sound incorrect if the grace notes are played with eighth note rhythms.

HOUSE OF THE RISING SUN

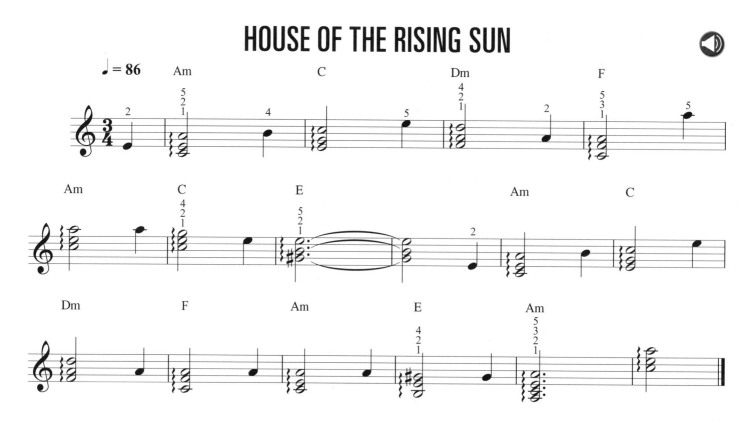

GLISSANDO

Another flashy effect we can create on the melodica is a glissando. A glissando has the player sliding from one key to another key and hitting all the white keys in between. The effect is a rapid succession of notes with a speed that would not be possible with traditional fingering. There is a unique technique used to achieve this sound: for an upward glissando, flip your hand over and use the flat part of your middle fingernail to glide up the keyboard. For a downward glissando, use the flat part of your thumbnail.

DARLENE

Putting it all together: the final song in this book uses many of the concepts we learned throughout including trills, melodic rolls, chord symbols, incomplete measures, 3/4 time signature, dynamics, vibrato, and more.

LAST NIGHT WAS THE LAST TIME

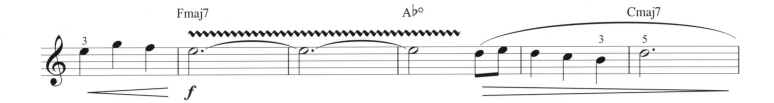

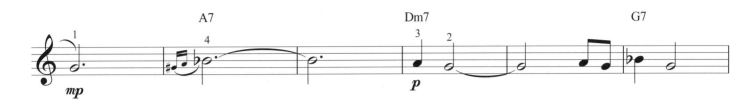

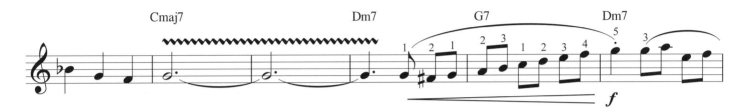

CHORD CHART

(×) = double sharp
(♭♭) = double flat